# 12-Bar Fingerstyle BLUES

## 25 Solo Pieces for Acoustic or Electric Guitar

### by Dave Rubin

Guitar: Doug Boduch

ISBN 978-1-4234-9080-7

HAL•LEONARD®
CORPORATION
7777 W. BLUEMOUND RD. P.O. BOX 13819 MILWAUKEE, WI 53213

In Australia Contact:
**Hal Leonard Australia Pty. Ltd.**
4 Lentara Court
Cheltenham, Victoria, 3192 Australia
Email: ausadmin@halleonard.com.au

Visit Hal Leonard Online at
**www.halleonard.com**

# CONTENTS

# The Guitar in the Blues: 1860–1920

The steel-string flat top guitar has been the iconic instrument of the blues only since the early 20th century. However, the roots of the gut-string acoustic guitar in the U.S. lead back to Spanish explorers in the southwest and the British colonizers in the east who brought them to the New World. Civil War guitars were readily available in the north and when Union soldiers left some behind in the south in the 1860s, a number found their way into the hands of freed slaves. Up until that time American blacks had been playing the banjo (or "banjar" or "banzar"), a true American instrument, with roots in North Africa as the Arab "bania," that evolved from a gourd with a stick and strings. The banjo and its close relative the tenor banjo were apparently tuned lower in early blues than would become the standard in folk and country music. Nonetheless, the deeper, fuller sound and sustain of the six-string guitar would eventually make it the solo instrument of choice by the twenties for accompanying the early blues musicians as it gained ascendance over the banjo and the mandolin.

# Dedication

I would like to dedicate this book to a true bluesman and valued friend, Zeke Shein of Matt Umanov Guitars on Bleecker Street in Greenwich Village.

# A Note on the Transcriptions

Many prewar and postwar fingerstyle blues are in open tunings. In the interest of accessibility and efficiency, I have opted to present all musical figures in standard tuning.

Dave Rubin
New York City, 2010

# About the Audio

Recorded, mixed, and mastered by Doug Boduch.

# Delta and Southern Country Blues

**S**ylvester Weaver (1897–1960) from Kentucky was the first "guitar hero" and the first African American to accompany a blues singer when he backed Sara Martin in 1923. Two weeks after that session, he also became the first black man to wax the instrumentals "Guitar Blues" and "Guitar Rag."

Lonnie Johnson (1894–1970) is rightly considered by many to be the most important guitarist of the 20th century, having been a pioneer single-string soloist in jazz and blues. His professional career commenced in 1925 playing Dixieland jazz with Louis Armstrong, but he also recorded solo 12-bar country blues like "Lifesaver Blues" in 1927, which were harmonically and melodically more sophisticated than that of his peers. He returned to playing solo guitar right up until his death.

The figurative (if not literal) "Founder of the Delta Blues" was Charlie Patton (1885–1934). He likely began playing guitar in the early 1890s on fabled Dockery Plantation in the Mississippi Delta and recorded classics like "Pony Blues," "Bo Weavil Blues," "Spoonful Blues," "Screamin' and Hollerin' the Blues" (released as the "Masked Marvel"), and "High Water Everywhere" in 1929. Rough as dry tree bark, he was the archetype of the tough, boozing, and brawling bluesman.

Skip James (1902–1969) is unique among the giants of Delta blues in that he performed his greatest work in the somber open D minor tuning. Following his monumental 1931 session that produced "Devil Got My Woman," "Hard Time Killing Floor Blues," "Cypress Grove Blues," "Illinois Blues," and "I'm So Glad," he would not record again until the mid-sixties. The latter song was famously and lucratively covered by Cream in 1968, with the royalties helping to pay for James' medical bills at the end of his life.

One of the most underappreciated of the blues playing "Johnsons," Tommy (1896–1956) exerted considerable influence on his peers. A world-class drinker even by blues standards when not out chasing women, he was known to imbibe shoe polish or sterno strained through bread if alcohol was unavailable; he celebrated the latter in "Canned Heat Blues." His other classics recorded in 1928–29 include the immortal "Big Road Blues."

The most famous Delta blues artist is Robert Johnson (1911–1938), an exceedingly talented guitarist, singer, and songwriter. The attention paid to his haunting lyrics and supposed "deal with the devil" at the "crossroads" sometimes tends to obscure his enormous musical achievement. Coming as it did at the end of the Delta blues era in 1936–37, his 29 known compositions represent a summing up of all that went before, though the cut boogie patterns of "Sweet Home Chicago" and "Ramblin' on My Mind" forecast the prime rhythm of postwar electric blues and rock 'n' roll.

The "Boogie Man," John Lee Hooker (1917–2001), helped usher in the era of postwar electric blues in Detroit in 1948 as did Muddy Waters in Chicago. However, the long roots of his unique, groundbreaking style wind their way back to the prewar Mississippi Delta. His first recording, the epochal "Boogie Chillun," reportedly sold one million copies and is the original source for every subsequent guitar boogie in blues and rock. Hooker followed with more "endless" boogies as well as "Crawling King Snake," "Maudie," and "Blues Before Sunrise," among many other classics.

 **TRACK 1**

Moderately ♩ = 80 (♫ = ♩³♪)

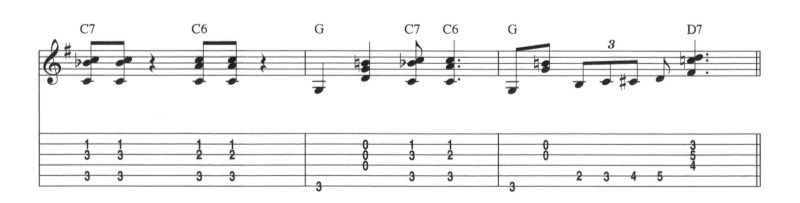

**Moderately slow** ♩ = 69 ( ♫ = ♩♪ )

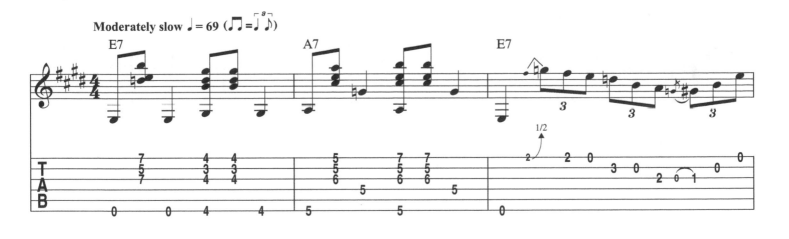

**TRACK 3**

Moderately ♩ = 88 (♫ = ♩♪)

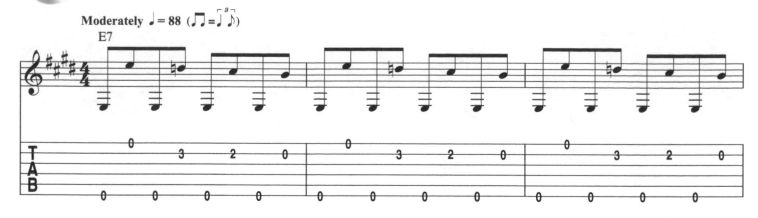

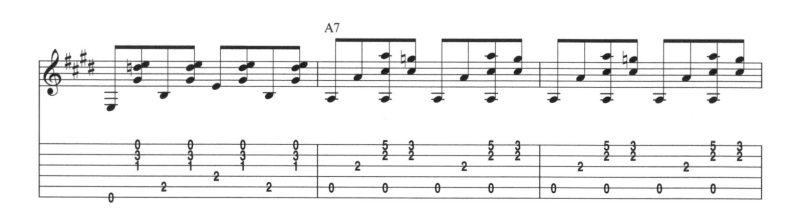

Moderately ♩ = 88

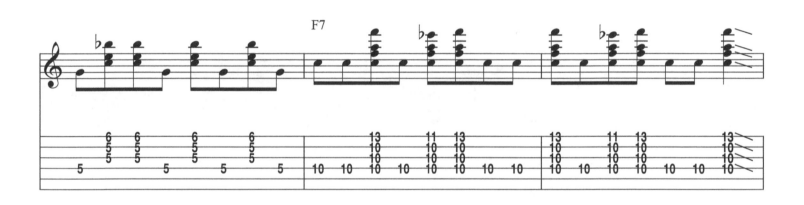

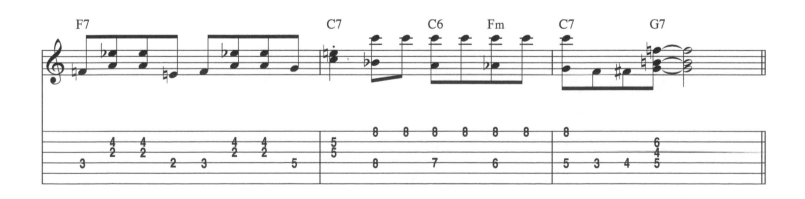

9

**Moderately** ♩ = 96 ( ♫ = ♪³♪ )

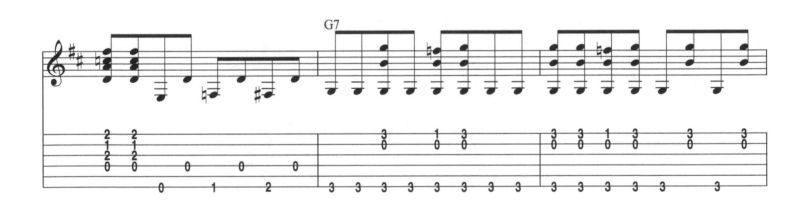

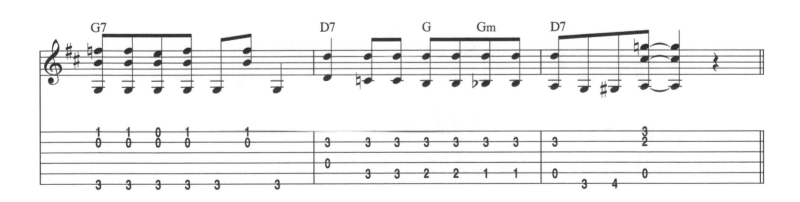

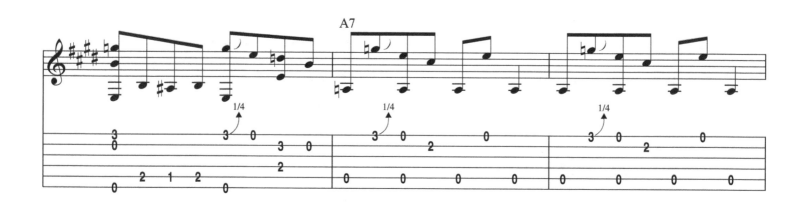

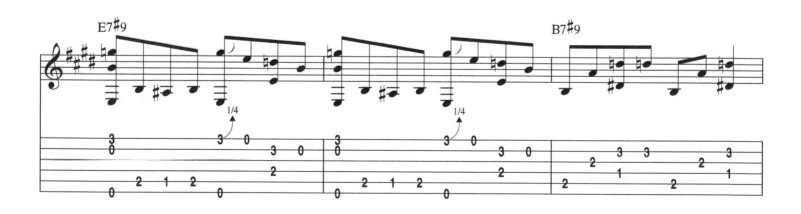

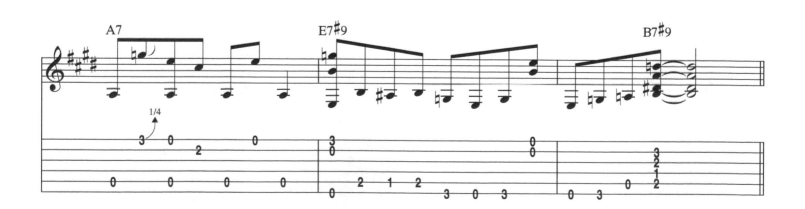

TRACK 8

Moderately ♩ = 80 ( ♫ = ♩♪ )

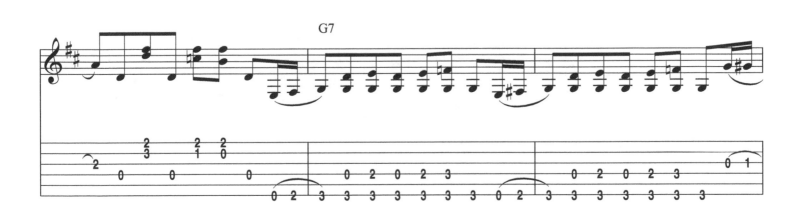

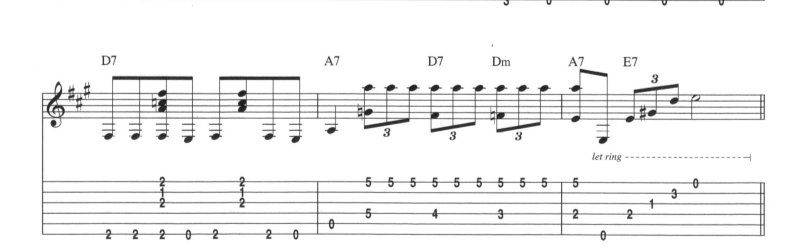

Moderately ♩ = 76

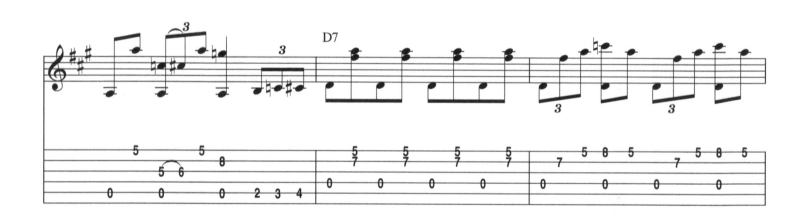

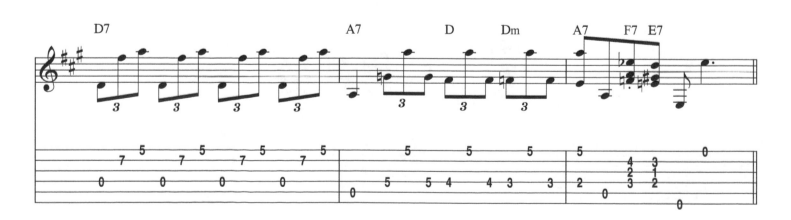

Moderately ♩ = 92 (♫ = ♩♪ )

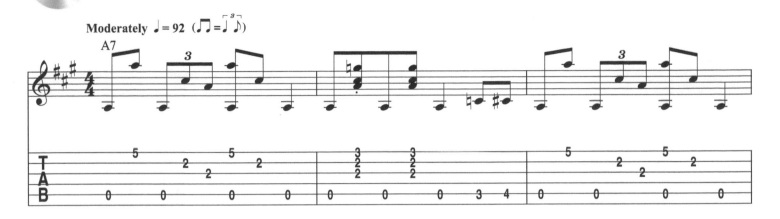

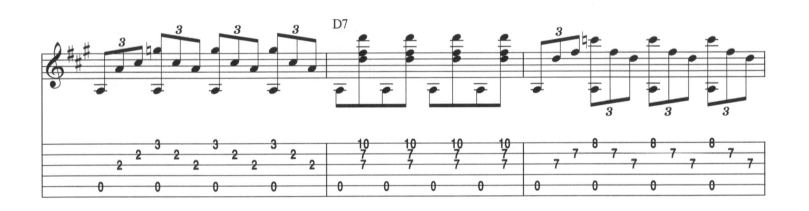

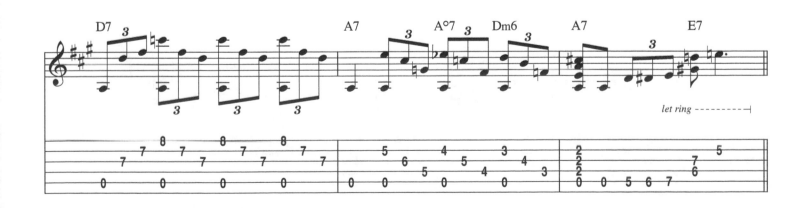

**Fast Boogie** ♩ = 152 (♫ = ♪♪)

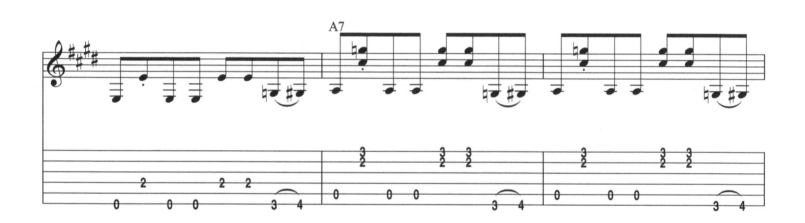

# Ragtime Blues

**M**ississippi John Hurt (1893–1966) was born in the north Mississippi hill country and played in a lighter, lyrical style derived from ragtime that avoided the driving, chugging riffs and bottleneck guitar of Delta blues. He initially recorded in 1927–28, producing "Candy Man Blues," "Stack O'Lee Blues," Louis Collins," and "Avalon Blues." It was the latter that led to his "rediscovery" when he was tracked down by a blues scholar in his hometown of Avalon, Mississippi in 1963.

Huddie "Lead Belly" Ledbetter (1888–1949) led a more romantic blues life than could be imagined. Born in Louisiana, he became proficient on the piano, mandolin, harmonica, violin, and accordion, though he is most known as "King of the 12-String Guitar." He was imprisoned in 1918, 1930, and 1939 and was released the first time after writing a song for the warden. His huge repertoire includes a wide range of classic material including "Goodnight, Irene," "Midnight Special," "Rock Island Line," and "Black Betty."

# Piedmont Blues

**P**iedmont blues refers to a style that flourished in the southeastern U.S. between the two world wars and is closer to ragtime than Delta blues in its alternating bass patterns. Blind Blake and Blind Willie McTell were two of its most famous practitioners. Blake (1895–1936), the "King of Ragtime Guitar" from Georgia, was a virtuoso whose style closely resembles ragtime piano—most notably heard in "Georgia Bound" and "Black Dog Blues." McTell (1903–1959), also from Georgia, is best known for "Statesboro Blues" as recorded by the Allman Brothers Band, but his unparalleled excellence on the 12-string guitar extended to many other compositions, including "Broke Down Engine." His influence extends far beyond the blues to Bob Dylan, Jack White, and even Kurt Cobain.

 TRACK 15

TRACK 16

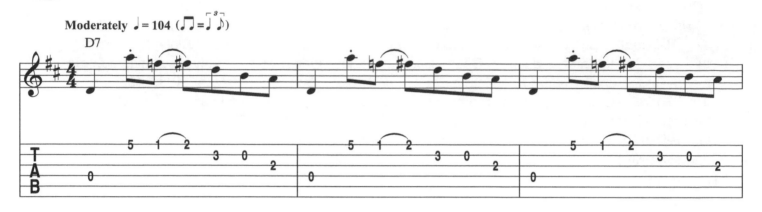

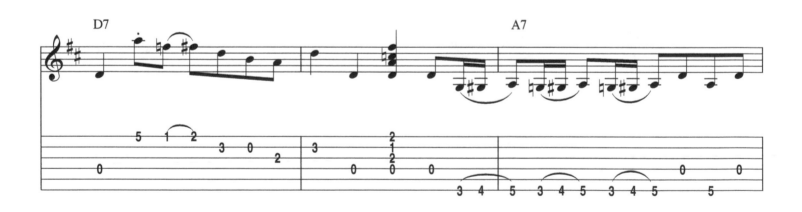

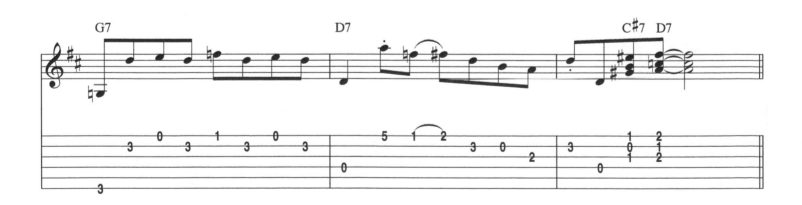

# Prewar Chicago Blues

**B**ig Bill Broonzy (1893–1958) and Memphis Minnie (1897–1973), along with the slide wizard Tampa Red (1904–1981), constitute the "big three" of acoustic prewar Chicago blues. Broonzy had an exceptionally long and productive career. Though like McTell he's best known for a song covered by electric blues guitarists ("Key to the Highway"), he left a large catalog and is also remembered for performing in place of the late Robert Johnson at Carnegie Hall in 1938.

Minnie made her mark by beating both Broonzy and Red in a "cutting contest" and is the first female blues guitar hero. She too, unfortunately, is best remembered among rock fans for "When the Levee Breaks" as imaginatively interpreted by Led Zeppelin. She contributed many other classics, however, including "Moaning Blues" and the slyly risqué "Me and My Chauffeur Blues."

**TRACK 17**

TRACK 18

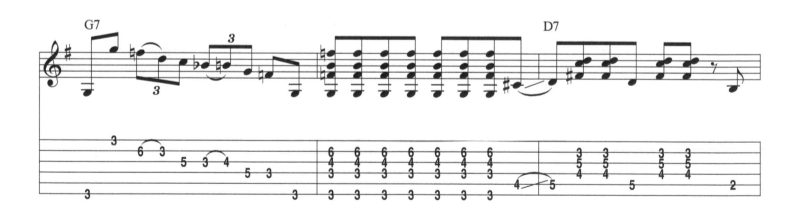

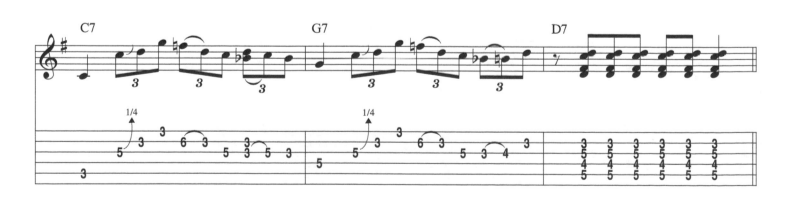

24

# Texas Blues

**B**lind Lemon Jefferson (1893–1929) was not only the first virtuoso guitar picker who salted his blues with numerous single-note fills, but the first acknowledged commercial blues star. His recordings of "Black Snake Moan" and "Matchbox Blues" in 1926 virtually began the era of country blues. Like Jimi Hendrix, his career was cut short after only three years.

One of Jefferson's esteemed followers was Lightnin' Hopkins (1912–1982) who actually met and played with the master in the twenties. Equally adept on acoustic or electric guitar, he began his recording career in 1946. Like John Lee Hooker, he would eventually record over 100 albums, including his early classics "Hello Central" and "Coffee Blues."

TRACK 19

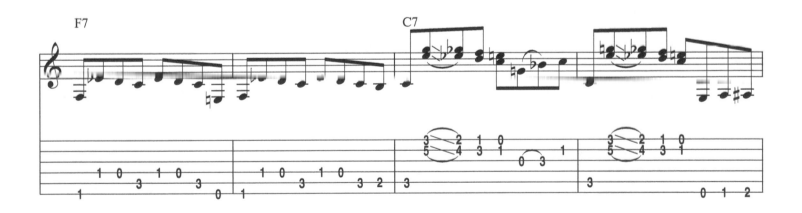

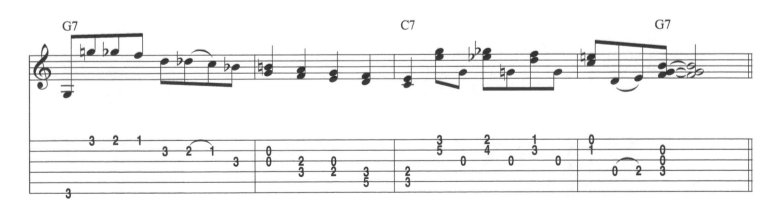

Slow Blues ♩ = 69

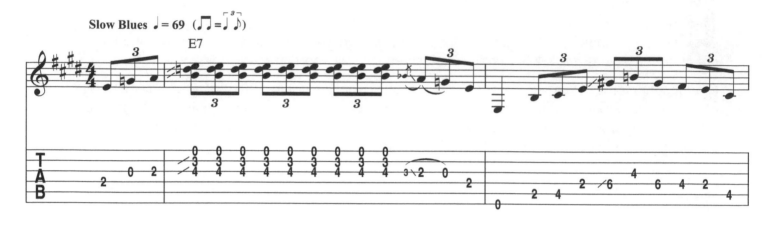

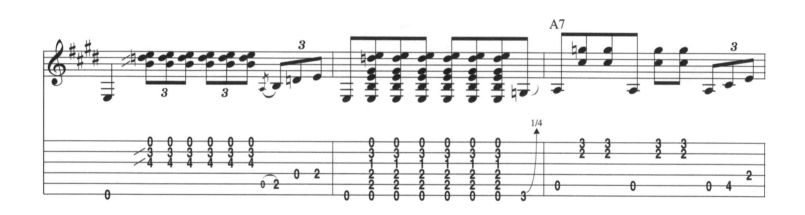

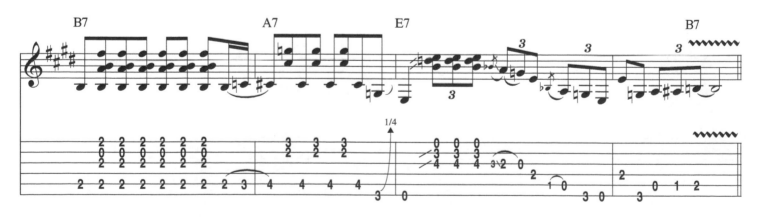

# Postwar Chicago Blues

Though not literally the first to play electric blues in Chicago after WWII, Muddy Waters (1915–1983) is rightly recognized as the one to bring electrified country blues to the fore. In 1948, he recorded "Can't Be Satisfied" b/w "Feel Like Going Home" and initiated a new era in the blues while going on to add a long list of classics, such as "Rollin' Stone," "Hoochie Coochie Man," "Mannish Boy," and "Got My Mojo Working."

 TRACK 21

TRACK 22

**Slow Blues** ♩ = 69 (♫ = ♩♪)

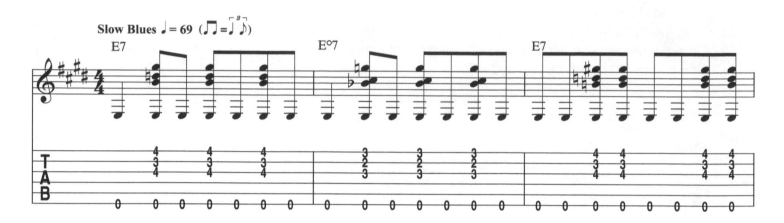

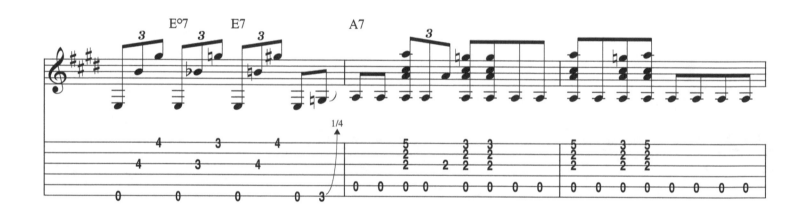

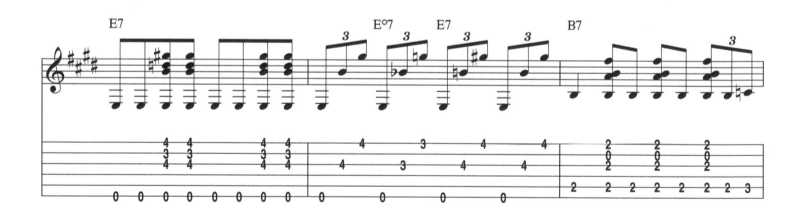

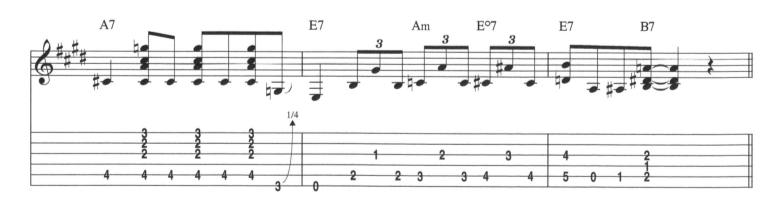

28

Uptempo Boogie ♩ = 142

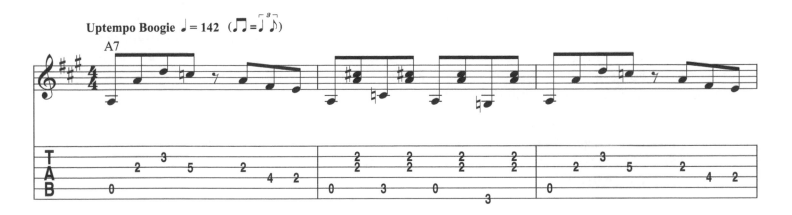

# Modern American Solo Steel-String Blues

The musically innovative sixties saw the evolution of folk guitar into a subgenre of exceptionally talented, eclectic artists that drew on country blues as a primary source of inspiration. John Fahey (1939–2001) was the eccentric figurehead of the movement and a recognized blues scholar. Testament to the former is his early pseudonym of "Blind Joe Death," and the latter his college thesis on Charlie Patton. Epic tracks like "The Great San Bernardino Birthday Party" combine elements of country blues, Indian ragas, and psychedelia.

Leo Kottke (born 1945), the musical heir of Fahey, is arguably the most virtuosic and creative of the group that includes Robbie Basho, Duck Baker, and Stefan Grossman, among others. His *6 and 12 String Guitar* from 1969 remains a landmark and the benchmark of devastatingly advanced fingerstyle guitar.

 TRACK 24

30

**Uptempo Boogie** ♩ = 112

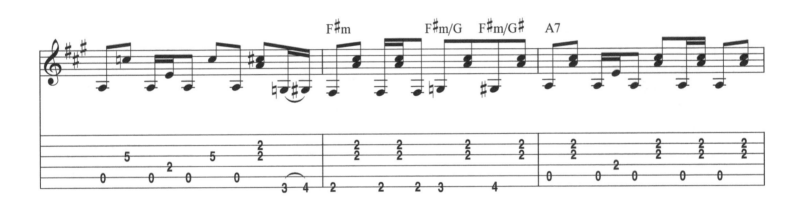

# Guitar Notation Legend

Guitar music can be notated three different ways: on a *musical staff*, in *tablature*, and in *rhythm slashes*.

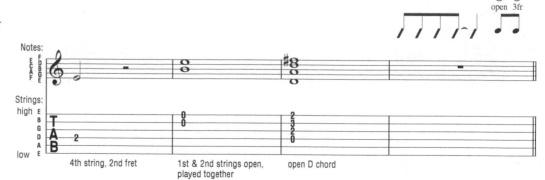

**RHYTHM SLASHES** are written above the staff. Strum chords in the rhythm indicated. Use the chord diagrams found at the top of the first page of the transcription for the appropriate chord voicings. Round noteheads indicate single notes.

**THE MUSICAL STAFF** shows pitches and rhythms and is divided by bar lines into measures. Pitches are named after the first seven letters of the alphabet.

**TABLATURE** graphically represents the guitar fingerboard. Each horizontal line represents a string, and each number represents a fret.

4th string, 2nd fret · 1st & 2nd strings open, played together · open D chord

**HALF-STEP BEND:** Strike the note and bend up 1/2 step.

**WHOLE-STEP BEND:** Strike the note and bend up one step.

**GRACE NOTE BEND:** Strike the note and immediately bend up as indicated.

**SLIGHT (MICROTONE) BEND:** Strike the note and bend up 1/4 step.

**BEND AND RELEASE:** Strike the note and bend up as indicated, then release back to the original note. Only the first note is struck.

**PRE-BEND:** Bend the note as indicated, then strike it.

**VIBRATO:** The string is vibrated by rapidly bending and releasing the note with the fretting hand.

**WIDE VIBRATO:** The pitch is varied to a greater degree by vibrating with the fretting hand.

**HAMMER-ON:** Strike the first (lower) note with one finger, then sound the higher note (on the same string) with another finger by fretting it without picking.

**PULL-OFF:** Place both fingers on the notes to be sounded. Strike the first note and without picking, pull the finger off to sound the second (lower) note.

**LEGATO SLIDE:** Strike the first note and then slide the same fret-hand finger up or down to the second note. The second note is not struck.

**SHIFT SLIDE:** Same as legato slide, except the second note is struck.

**TRILL:** Very rapidly alternate between the notes indicated by continuously hammering on and pulling off.

**TAPPING:** Hammer ("tap") the fret indicated with the pick-hand index or middle finger and pull off to the note fretted by the fret hand.

**NATURAL HARMONIC:** Strike the note while the fret-hand lightly touches the string directly over the fret indicated.

**PINCH HARMONIC:** The note is fretted normally and a harmonic is produced by adding the edge of the thumb or the tip of the index finger of the pick hand to the normal pick attack.

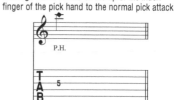

**PICK SCRAPE:** The edge of the pick is rubbed down (or up) the string, producing a scratchy sound.

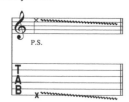

**MUFFLED STRINGS:** A percussive sound is produced by laying the fret hand across the string(s) without depressing, and striking them with the pick hand.

**PALM MUTING:** The note is partially muted by the pick hand lightly touching the string(s) just before the bridge.

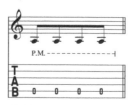

**RAKE:** Drag the pick across the strings indicated with a single motion.

**TREMOLO PICKING:** The note is picked as rapidly and continuously as possible.

**VIBRATO BAR DIVE AND RETURN:** The pitch of the note or chord is dropped a specified number of steps (in rhythm), then returned to the original pitch.

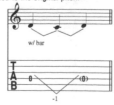

**VIBRATO BAR SCOOP:** Depress the bar just before striking the note, then quickly release the bar.

**VIBRATO BAR DIP:** Strike the note and then immediately drop a specified number of steps, then release back to the original pitch.